PLATE TECTONICS

JULIA J. QUINLAN

Britannica
Educational Publishing

IN ASSOCIATION WITH

ROSEN
EDUCATIONAL SERVICES

Published in 2018 by Britannica Educational Publishing (a trademark of Encyclopædia Britannica, Inc.) in association with The Rosen Publishing Group, Inc.
29 East 21st Street, New York, NY 10010

Distributed exclusively by Rosen Publishing.
To see additional Britannica Educational Publishing titles, go to rosenpublishing.com.

First Edition

Britannica Educational Publishing
J.E. Luebering: Executive Director, Core Editorial
Mary Rose McCudden: Editor, Britannica Student Encyclopedia

Rosen Publishing
Amelie von Zumbusch: Editor
Nelson Sá: Art Director
Nicole Russo-Duca: Designer & Book Layout
Cindy Reiman: Photography Manager
Ellina Litmanovich: Photo Researcher

Library of Congress Cataloging-in-Publication Data

Names: Quinlan, Julia J., author.
Title: Plate tectonics / Julia J. Quinlan.
Description: New York : Britannica Educational Publishing in Association with Rosen Educational Services, 2018. | Series: Let's find out! Our dynamic earth | Audience: Grades 1–4. | Includes bibliographical references and index.
Identifiers: LCCN 2017016035| ISBN 9781680488333 (library bound : alk. paper) | ISBN 9781680488326 (pbk. : alk. paper) | ISBN 9781538300299 (6 pack : alk. paper)
Subjects: LCSH: Plate tectonics—Juvenile literature. | Geology—History—Juvenile literature. | Earth sciences—Juvenile literature.
Classification: LCC QE511.4 .Q85 2018 | DDC 551.1/36—dc23
LC record available at https://lccn.loc.gov/2017016035

Manufactured in the United States of America

Photo credits: Cover Andrea Danti/Shutterstock.com; pp. 4, 6, 7, 8, 12, 14, 16, 18, 19, 25, 28 © Encyclopædia Britannica, Inc.; p. 5 © tomas/Fotolia; p. 9 © Brian A. Vikander/West Light; p. 10 © G. Ziesler/Peter Arnold, Inc.; p. 11 Lonely Planet/Lonely Planet Images/Getty Images; p. 13 © NOAA; p. 15 © J. D. Grigg/USGS; p. 17 © USGS; p. 20 Walter Myers/Stocktrek Images/Getty Images; p. 21 WerksMedia/iStock/Thinkstock; p. 22 © Dennis Jacobsen/Fotolia; p. 23 Anton Balazh/Shutterstock.com; p. 24 © sdbower/Fotolia; p. 26 © Photos.com/Jupiterimages; p. 27 Ken Lucas/Visuals Unlimited/Getty Images; p. 29 Yannick Tylle/Corbis Documentary/Getty Images; back cover and interior pages background © iStockphoto.com/Joe_Potato.

CONTENTS

EARTH'S PLATES AND THEIR MOVEMENTS

As we go about our daily lives, Earth feels firm beneath our feet. It may come as a surprise that Earth is really covered in plates that are slowly moving. Earth is covered in a rigid outer layer, called the lithosphere. Under the lithosphere is a soft layer of melted rock called the asthenosphere. The lithosphere is broken up into about a dozen large plates and several small plates. These plates move slowly,

As you can see from this map, Earth's plates are a mix of different sizes and shapes.

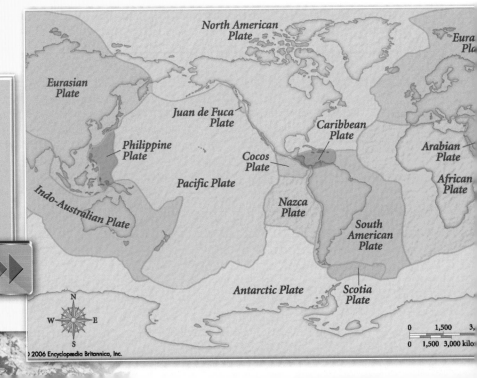

North American Plate

Eurasian Plate

Eurasian Plate

Juan de Fuca Plate

Philippine Plate

Caribbean Plate

Arabian Plate

African Plate

Cocos Plate

Pacific Plate

Indo-Australian Plate

Nazca Plate

South American Plate

Antarctic Plate

Scotia Plate

N
W E
S

0   1,500   3,
0   1,500   3,000 kilo

© 2006 Encyclopædia Britannica, Inc.

The Himalayas are a mountain range in Asia. They were formed by plate movements.

only about 2 to 4 inches (5 to 10 centimeters) per year.

The movements of these plates have a huge effect on our planet. Sudden plate movements can cause earthquakes. The movements of the plates can also form mountains and volcanoes. Over long spans of time, the movement of the plates—known as plate tectonics—can change the shape of continents and oceans. Scientists study plate tectonics to better understand the history of our planet.

THINK ABOUT IT

Do you think it takes hundreds, thousands, or millions of years for a mountain to form?

EARTH'S LAYERS

Earth's surface layer is a crust of solid rock. The crust is thinner under the oceans than it is under the continents. Under the continents it averages about 19 miles (30 km) thick. Underneath the crust is the more compact rock of the mantle, on which the crust basically floats. The mantle is much thicker, about 1,800 miles (2,900 km). The temperature at the lower part of the mantle is about 6,700°F (3,700°C). The rock there is soft and can move slowly. Below the mantle is Earth's core.

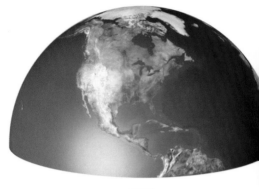

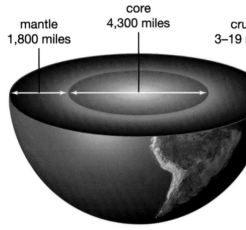

mantle
1,800 miles

core
4,300 miles

crus
3–19 m

© 2014 Encyclopædia Britannica, Inc.

This diagram shows Earth's three layers. As you can see, the crust is by far the thinnest layer.

The asthenosphere includes parts of the upper mantle. It is under the lithosphere and above the lower mantle.

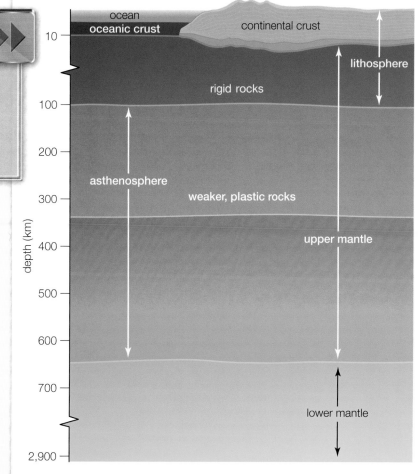

The outer part of the core is liquid, while the center of the core is solid.

The lithosphere consists of the crust and the rigid upper mantle. The asthenosphere is the partially **molten** zone in the mantle, between 60 and 400 miles (100 and 650 km) below the surface. The tectonic plates slide across the top of the asthenosphere.

VOCABULARY

Molten things have been melted, often by great heat.

7

DIVERGENT BOUNDARIES

Tectonic plates interact with each other in several ways. One way is to move away from each other. Plates that move apart are said to have a **divergent** boundary. When

The red on this map shows new crust, a sign that seafloor spreading is happening.

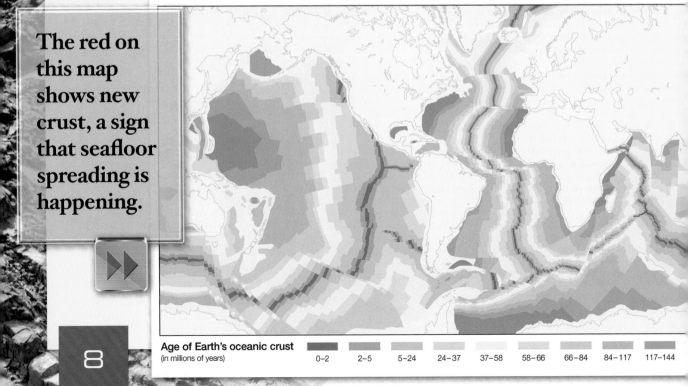

Age of Earth's oceanic crust
(in millions of years)

| 0–2 | 2–5 | 5–24 | 24–37 | 37–58 | 58–66 | 66–84 | 84–117 | 117–144 |

plates move apart they make a crack between them. When a crack opens up on the seafloor, magma rises up and fills in the crack. This is called seafloor spreading. This process can cause earthquakes in the ocean as the seafloor cracks, fills in, and cracks again.

Divergent boundaries can also exist on land and can create cracks in Earth's surface. These cracks are called rift valleys. The longest rift on Earth's surface is called the Great Rift Valley. It is about 4,000 miles (6,400 km) long with an average width of 30 to 40 miles (50 to 65 km). The rift starts in the Middle Eastern country of Jordan and goes south to the African country Mozambique.

In the background of this photograph you can see the cliffs of the Great Rift Valley in Kenya.

CONVERGENT BOUNDARIES

Plates that move toward each other have convergent boundaries. Usually, one of the plates ends up going underneath the other one. When this happens, the area around the two plates is called a subduction zone. There is a plate in the Pacific Ocean, the Nazca Plate, that is pushing under a plate that makes up South America.

As the Nazca Plate pushes under the South American plate, it presses into the hot mantle and melts rock, making magma. The magma rises up and causes the volcanoes on the Andes Mountains to form. This type of plate

The Andes run through the South American countries of Venezuela, Colombia, Ecuador, Peru, Bolivia, Argentina, and Chile.

COMPARE AND CONTRAST

The Andes are the longest chain of mountains in the world. They were formed by subduction. The Himalayas, the highest mountains on Earth, were formed by convergence. How might the way they formed have affected their length or height?

movement can also cause powerful earthquakes.

If two plates converge under the ocean, they can create volcanic islands. That is how the Mariana Islands in the western Pacific Ocean formed. When two plates on a continent converge, they can create mountains. That is how the Himalayas were created.

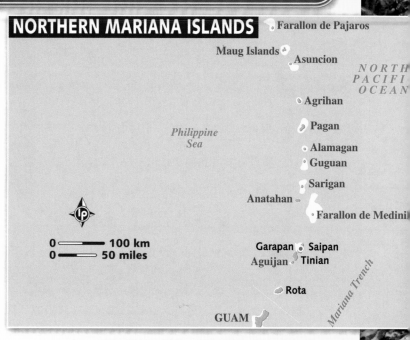

NORTHERN MARIANA ISLANDS

Farallon de Pajaros
Maug Islands
Asuncion
NORTH PACIFIC OCEAN
Agrihan
Philippine Sea
Pagan
Alamagan
Guguan
Sarigan
Anatahan
Farallon de Medinil
Garapan · Saipan
Aguijan · Tinian
Rota
Mariana Trench
GUAM

0 —— 100 km
0 —— 50 miles

The Mariana Islands lie on the border between the Pacific and Philippine Plates.

11

Transform Faults

The plates that make up transform faults do not push into each other or move away from each other. They slide past each other. Sometimes, the plates stick together and then slip. This causes earthquakes. Most transform faults are found on the ocean floor. Some, such as the San Andreas Fault in California, appear on continents.

The San Andreas Fault is more than 800 miles (1,300 km) long. The movement of the plates along the fault has caused several major earthquakes. A strong earthquake damaged much of the city of San

The San Andreas Fault extends for hundreds of miles through the state of California.

San Francisco was devastated by a massive earthquake that struck on April 18, 1906.

Francisco in 1906. Another strong earthquake struck the San Francisco area in 1989. Most of the population of California lives near the San Andreas Fault. Some cities and towns are built on top of the fault. Because of the fault, minor earthquakes and tremors are common in California. Buildings, roads, and bridges are built to be able to withstand these movements.

Think About It

The 1906 earthquake in San Francisco destroyed about 80 percent of the city. The 1989 earthquake was much less devastating. What improvements do you think made the city better prepared for earthquakes?

Volcanoes and Hot Spots

Volcanoes are mostly found along the boundaries of tectonic plates. They can be found on convergent boundaries and divergent boundaries. There are more than 1,500 volcanoes on Earth that could be active. Almost 90 percent of those volcanoes are located in the Pacific Ring of Fire. This is a chain of volcanoes that surrounds the Pacific Ocean. It lies along the edges of the

About 90 percent of all volcanoes are located along the Ring of Fire.

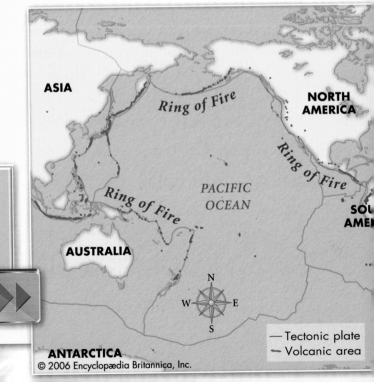

ASIA

Ring of Fire

NORTH AMERICA

Ring of Fire

Ring of Fire

PACIFIC OCEAN

SOU AME

AUSTRALIA

N

W   E

S

ANTARCTICA

© 2006 Encyclopædia Britannica, Inc.

—— Tectonic plate
—— Volcanic area

A volcano called Kilauea erupts in the Hawai'i Volcanoes National Park.

giant Pacific Plate. As the plate moves, it creates earthquakes and volcanoes.

While most volcanoes are found along tectonic plate boundaries, some are not. Some volcanoes can be found toward the center of tectonic plates. These volcanoes form over what scientists call a hot spot. A hot spot is an area where heat pushes up from Earth's mantle and melts the rock, creating magma, at the base of the lithosphere. The magma then pushes up through the crust, making volcanoes. This is how the Hawaiian Islands were created.

THINK ABOUT IT

Mauna Loa is the largest volcano on Earth. It is located in Hawaii. Can you name any other famous volcanoes?

EARTHQUAKES

Earthquakes happen every day all over the world. Most earthquakes are so small that people cannot feel them. Sometimes, larger earthquakes happen and they can cause serious damage. Most earthquakes are caused by the movement of tectonic plates. When plates move in relation to each other, they build up pressure. When the pressure becomes too great, the plates can move suddenly. This causes an earthquake. The energy is released in the form of shock waves. The waves spread through the rock

Earthquakes can be felt over a wide area.

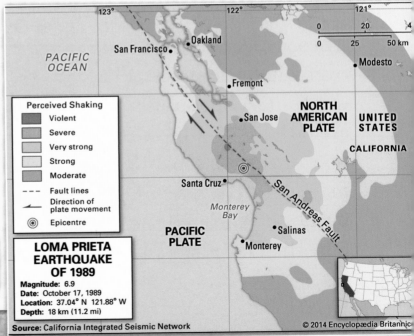

Perceived Shaking
- Violent
- Severe
- Very strong
- Strong
- Moderate
- - - - Fault lines
- Direction of plate movement
- ◎ Epicentre

LOMA PRIETA EARTHQUAKE OF 1989
Magnitude: 6.9
Date: October 17, 1989
Location: 37.04° N 121.88° W
Depth: 18 km (11.2 mi)

Source: California Integrated Seismic Network

© 2014 Encyclopædia Britannica

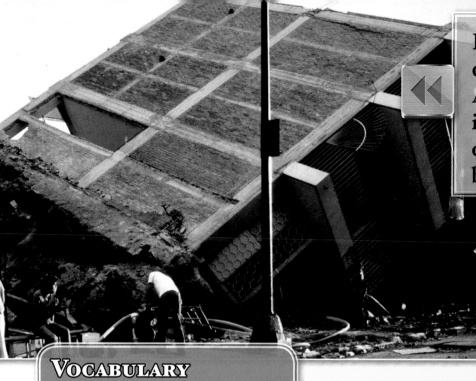

Earthquakes can do serious damage. A 1985 earthquake in Mexico City destroyed many buildings.

in all directions. In the most powerful quakes, people thousands of miles away from the center of the quake can feel the ground shake.

Earthquakes can do great damage to buildings, bridges, railroads, and other structures. The violent shaking during earthquakes often causes other problems as well, such as avalanches. Some quakes that happen in or near oceans cause huge, destructive waves called tsunamis to sweep ashore.

VOCABULARY

Avalanches are large amounts of snow and ice that fall down a mountainside or cliff.

Changing Continents

Plates have moved across Earth's surface for hundreds of millions of years. As the plates move, the continents on them move, too. This movement is called continental drift. The movement of the tectonic plates has changed the shape, size, and location of the continents.

About 255 million years ago, nearly all the land on Earth formed one enormous continent called Pangaea. This "supercontinent" began to break apart about 237 million years ago. By about 150

The arrows on this map show the ways in which the different plates are moving.

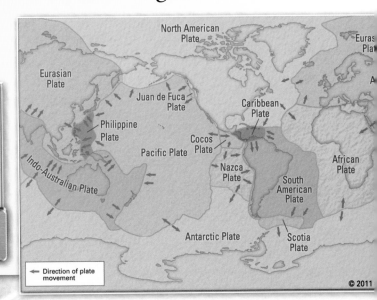

The continents have shifted greatly over the past 225 million years.

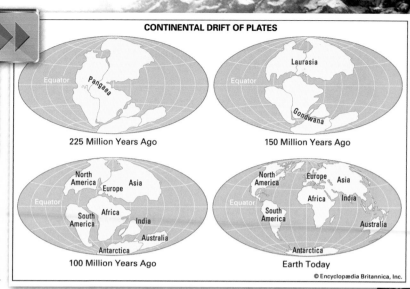

CONTINENTAL DRIFT OF PLATES

Equator — Pangaea — 225 Million Years Ago

Equator — Laurasia — Gondwana — 150 Million Years Ago

North America — Asia — Europe — South America — Africa — India — Australia — Antarctica — Equator — 100 Million Years Ago

North America — Europe — Asia — Africa — India — South America — Australia — Antarctica — Equator — Earth Today

© Encyclopædia Britannica, Inc.

million years ago, it had separated into two large landmasses, Laurasia in the north and Gondwana in the south. Laurasia was made up of the land that is now North America, Europe, and much of Asia. Gondwana included what are now South America, Africa, Australia, Antarctica, India, and Arabia. Later, Laurasia and Gondwana split into pieces. Gondwana began to break apart about 180 million years ago and Laurasia broke apart about 50 million years ago.

THINK ABOUT IT

North America is moving west at about an inch (3 cm) per year. What do you think is pushing North America west?

Scientists believe that this process has happened several times over Earth's long history. They think that it takes about 500 million years for all the continents to join together into one big continent and then break apart again. The continents continue to move today. Scientists believe that in about 250 million years they will join together again.

The idea of continental drift is an old one. It was first suggested to explain why the shapes of the continents looked like they would fit

Scientists think a supercontinent called Pannotia existed 600 million years ago. It likely looked something like this.

together well. Besides the shape of the continents, there is much evidence supporting the idea that the continents were once united. Most of the evidence

is based on the study of ancient climates and the matching of fossils, rocks, and geological structures on land separated by huge oceans. For example, fossils of swimming reptiles called mesosaurs are found in both Africa and South America.

The Appalachian Mountains were once part of the same chain as mountains that are now in Scotland and Scandinavia.

EVOLUTION AND CLIMATE

The changing shapes and locations of continents has had an effect on the evolution of plants and animals. As the continents moved apart, the diversity, or differences, among plants and animals increased. This is because the spaces that opened up between the continents were filled in with ocean. That meant the plants and animals on different continents could not interact. This is why the animals that live in Australia, like kangaroos, are so different from the animals in North America, like grizzly bears.

Kangaroos exist only in Australia because there was no way for them to travel to other continents.

However, the movement of the plates had the opposite effect about three million years ago. At about that time, volcanic activity in the Pacific Ocean created a land bridge between North America and South America. This land bridge formed the Isthmus of Panama. Before that, the two continents were separated. This bridge allowed animals to migrate between the two continents.

The Isthmus of Panama is within the country of Panama. The Panama Canal crosses the isthmus.

Many animals from North America migrated south. Among those animals were many carnivorous,

or meat-eating, animals. These carnivores caused the extinction of some animals on the southern continent. Some southern animals, like the armadillo and opossum, migrated north.

The nine-banded armadillo is the only species of armadillo found in the United States.

Tectonic plates and their movements have also caused extinctions. About 299 to 252 million years ago, a series of extinction events happened. About 70 percent of land animals became extinct, and about 95 percent of marine animals became extinct. Scientists think this was caused by the formation of Pangaea, volcanic activity, and temperature changes.

The breakup of Pangaea also had a big effect on Earth's climate. A lot of the climate on Earth has to do with ocean currents and wind. When Pangaea existed,

THINK ABOUT IT

Why might carnivores that are new to an area cause the extinction of some animals?

it was completely surrounded by an ocean, called Panthalassa. As Pangaea split apart, the ocean filled in the gaps. This changed the currents and spread warm and cold water differently.

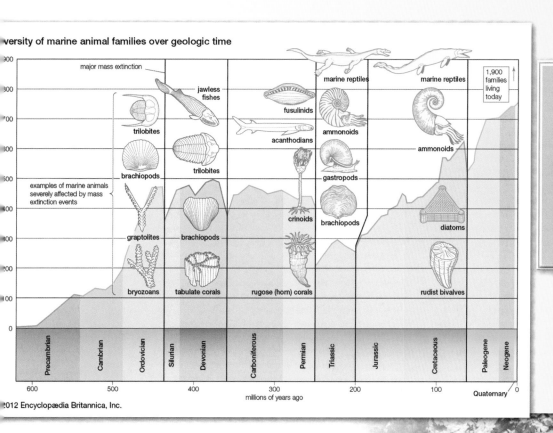

Diversity of marine animal families over geologic time

There have been mass extinctions throughout Earth's history.

DISCOVERING EARTH'S PLATES

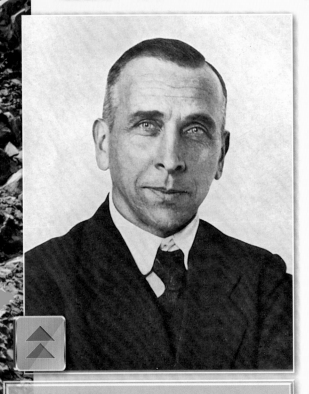

Alfred Wegener spent most of his life studying meteorology and geology.

In 1912, a German scientist named Alfred Wegener suggested that, at one time, all of the continents were joined together in a supercontinent called Pangaea. He thought that Pangaea split apart and the pieces drifted apart over long periods of time. He called this idea continental displacement. His **theory** is now called continental drift.

> **VOCABULARY**
>
> A scientific **theory** is an explanation for why things work or how things happen.

Fossils of the *Glossopteris* plant were some of the first evidence to support the idea of continental drift.

Other scientists rejected Wegener's idea because he could not explain how the continents moved.

In 1929, a British geologist named Arthur Holmes proposed that the heat from Earth's mantle caused continental drift. His idea received little attention at the time. In the 1960s, however, a number of scientists used the ideas of Holmes and Wegener. They monitored earthquakes and looked at similar fossils from different continents. By doing all of that, the scientists were able to find evidence of plates and their movements. The modern theory of plate tectonics was developed.

PLATE TECTONICS AND THE FUTURE

Earth's continents are always moving—slowly. Plate tectonics will continue to change the shape of the continents and oceans over the course of hundreds of millions of years. Most of the time, this slow movement doesn't affect our lives. However, when plates suddenly come together, slide against each other, or move apart, serious disasters can occur. Scientists think that it is only a matter of time before another large earthquake happens in California. The San Andreas Fault has been building up pressure for a long time there.

Earth's surface has been shaped by plate tectonics.

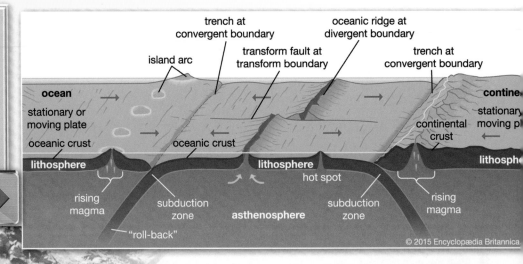

trench at convergent boundary

oceanic ridge at divergent boundary

island arc

transform fault at transform boundary

trench at convergent boundary

ocean

stationary or moving plate

continent

stationary or moving plate

oceanic crust

oceanic crust

continental crust

lithosphere

lithosphere

hot spot

lithosphere

rising magma

subduction zone

asthenosphere

subduction zone

rising magma

"roll-back"

© 2015 Encyclopædia Britannica

COMPARE AND CONTRAST

How are the threats from tsunamis and earthquakes different? How are they similar?

In the last decades, devastating tsunamis have occurred in Japan and Indonesia. The huge waves were caused by earthquakes. The earthquakes were triggered by plates on the ocean floor sliding under each other. The idea of earthquakes and tsunamis is scary. But scientists are improving how they monitor the movement of Earth's plates. This allows scientists to warn people about dangerous events before they occur.

This scientist is studying Mount Nyiragongo, a volcano in Africa's Great Rift Valley.

GLOSSARY

asthenosphere The layer of soft, molten rock that lies under the lithosphere.

boundary The dividing line or edge between things.

climate The average weather conditions of a particular place or region over a period of years.

continent One of the great divisions of land (North America, South America, Europe, Asia, Africa, Australia, and Antarctica) on the globe.

converge To tend or move toward one point or one another.

core The hot, inner layer of Earth.

crust Earth's thin, rocky outer layer.

displacement Movement from one position to another.

evolution An explanation for how all the kinds of living things that exist today developed from earlier types.

extinction No longer existing.

fault A break in Earth's crust accompanied by a displacement of rock masses parallel to the break.

geological Having to do with rocks and the history of rocks.

lithosphere The solid, outer part of Earth, consisting of the crust and part of the mantle.

magma Hot, melted rock material within Earth.

mantle The portion of Earth lying between the crust and the core.

migrate To move from one country, place, or location to another.

seafloor The floor of a sea or ocean.

shock wave A tall wave caused by a shock (as from an earthquake or explosion) to the material through which the wave travels.

subduction The process in which one tectonic plate is forced beneath the edge of another plate.

tremor A small movement of the ground before or after an earthquake.

tsunami A great sea wave produced especially by an earthquake or volcanic eruption under the sea.

volcano A vent in Earth's crust from which melted or hot rock and steam come out.

FOR MORE INFORMATION

Books

Brooks, Susie. *Earthquakes and Volcanoes* (Where on Earth?). New York, NY: PowerKids Press, 2017.

Elkins, Elizabeth. *Investigating Earthquakes* (Investigating Natural Disasters). North Mankato, MN: Capstone Press, 2017.

Greer, Eileen. *Plate Tectonics* (Spotlight on Earth Science). New York, NY: PowerKids Press, 2017.

Schuh, Mari C. *Tsunamis* (Earth in Action). North Mankato, MN: Capstone Press, 2016.

Winchester, Simon. *When the Earth Shakes: Earthquakes, Volcanoes, and Tsunamis*. New York, NY: Viking Books for Young Readers, 2015.

Websites

Because of the changing nature of internet links, Rosen Publishing has developed an online list of websites related to the subject of this book. This site is updated regularly. Please use this link to access the list:

http://www.rosenlinks.com/LFO/Plate

INDEX